Knit it

greeting cards

Margriet Kors
Gina Kors-Lambers

FORTE PUBLISHERS

Contents

ISBN 90 5877 461 9

This is a publication from
Forte Publishers BV
P.O. Box 1394
3500 BJ Utrecht
The Netherlands

For more information about the creative
books available from Forte Uitgevers:
www.forteuitgevers.nl

Final editing: Gina Kors-Lambers,
Steenwijk, the Netherlands
Photography and digital image editing:
Fotografie Gerhard Witteveen,
Apeldoorn, the Netherlands
Cover and inner design:
BADE creatieve communicatie, Baarn,
the Netherlands
Translation: Michael Ford, TextCase,
Hilversum, the Netherlands

Preface

If two people write a book about making cards and one person wants to cut and the other wants to tear, then what do you get? The answer is very pretty cards which you have never seen before. Combining cut and torn pieces of paper and sticking them together gives you a special basis with which to make cards. If you then also add miniature knitwear, you get a fantastic result. You can combine different types of paper to your heart's content, because there are so many different types. You can make romantic, tender or rugged cards as you wish.

So start knitting, cutting and tearing.

We wish you lots of fun making the knit it cards.

Gina   Margriet

Techniques

Knitwear

This book contains several different pieces of miniature knitwear. To make these, you need no. 2 knitting needles.

Small cloth

Cast on 15 stitches and knit 5.5 rows.

Sweater

Cast on 8 stitches, knit 7 rows and increase 5 stitches. Increase another 5 stitches after the 8th row. You will now have sleeves on the knitwear. Knit another 2.5 rows.

Scarf

Cast on 5 stitches and knit 15.5 rows.

Nappy

Cast on 3 stitches and increase one stitch every row. Knit 12 rows. Cast off the last row.

1. The materials for making knit it cards.

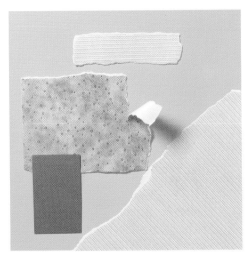
2. A combination of cut and torn pieces of paper.

3. Apply chalk to the edges of the torn pieces.

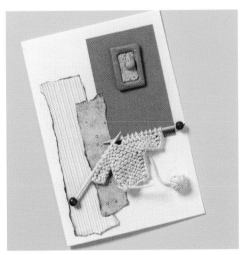
4. Stick all the paper and the knitwear on the card.

Finishing the knitting

Once you have finished the knitwear, cut off the cast-on yarn. Also cut off the knitting yarn so that it is 50 cm long. Place the knitwear on cocktail sticks, apply a small amount of Aleene's Thick Designer Tacky glue on the ends of the cocktail sticks and slide a wooden coloured bead (6 mm) on them. Roll up the long end of the yarn into a ball or wind it around a piece of card. Use Aleene's Thick Designer Tacky glue to stick the knitwear on the card.

Paper

Different types of paper are used in this book. It does not have to be difficult to find a good combination. Nowadays, there are many different packets and pads on the market which have good combinations of paper. The Sharon Ann packets consist of eight different types of pattern paper and two different types of vellum. There are also Little Sizzles are pads which have 80 sheets of pattern paper and plain paper in very pretty colours.

Tearing paper

Many people are scared to tear paper. There is no reason to be scared, though, because it cannot go wrong. The best thing about torn paper is the surprising white edges which often give the card a nice contrast. To make white edges, take a piece of paper in your left hand and tear the paper upwards with your right hand. For left-handed people, hold the paper in your right hand and tear with your left hand.

Chalks

You can leave the torn edges white, but you can also colour them using chalks. Chalks are coloured, compressed lime tablets. Apply a small amount of chalk to the applicator from the box and rub it over the torn edge of the paper moving away from the paper. It is also nice to use two or more different colours of chalk and have them overlap.

Materials

- Catania knitting yarn
- Inox knitting needles (no. 2)
- Cocktail sticks
- Make Me wooden beads (Ø 6 mm)
- Card: Cardstock (C) and Mi-Teintes (M)
- K & Company scrapbook paper
- Sharon Ann scrapbook paper
- Little Sizzles
- Scrap pads
- Decorating Chalks
- Make Me eyelet tags
- Make Me jewellery glue
- Make Me embellishments
- Wire & Wire
- Cutting mat
- Make Me design knife
- Make Me photo glue
- Ruler
- Rubber
- Aleene's Thick Designer Tacky glue

Sheep

What you need
- ❏ *Knitwear: pale green (0192) and lilac (0126)*
- ❏ *Card:*
    grass green (C3170) and soft lilac (C5020)
- ❏ *Little Sizzles: Pastels and Watercolors*

Card 1

Extra materials
- ❏ *Scrap Pads: Bright kids*
- ❏ *Felt: light grey*
- ❏ *Tuft of wool*
- ❏ *Sizzix die cutter*
- ❏ *Sizzix die: sheep*

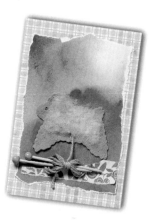

Make a soft lilac double card (10.5 x 15 cm). Cut a rectangle (9 x 13 cm) out of checked paper. Tear a rectangle (7.5 x 11 cm) out of rainbow paper and a strip (1 x 7.5 cm) out of rose paper. Stick the checked paper on the card and stick the rainbow paper and the rose paper on top. Make a sheep and stick this on the card together with a twine of lilac cotton and two knitting needles.

Card 2

Extra materials
- ❏ *Scrap Pads: Little princess and Bright kids*
- ❏ *Scrapbook basics: Farm animals*

Make a soft lilac double card (13 x 13 cm). Tear a square (12 x 12 cm) out of ivory card and apply chalk to the edges. Cut a square (11 x 11 cm) out of flower paper, a rectangle (6 x 10 cm) out of checked paper and a rectangle (3 x 8 cm) out of rainbow paper. Tear a strip (2 x 7 cm) out of green paper. Stick the ivory card on the card and stick the flower paper on top. Stick the rainbow paper and the green paper on the checked paper, and stick that on the flower paper. Stick the piece of pale green knitwear on the card and stick the Charm on top.

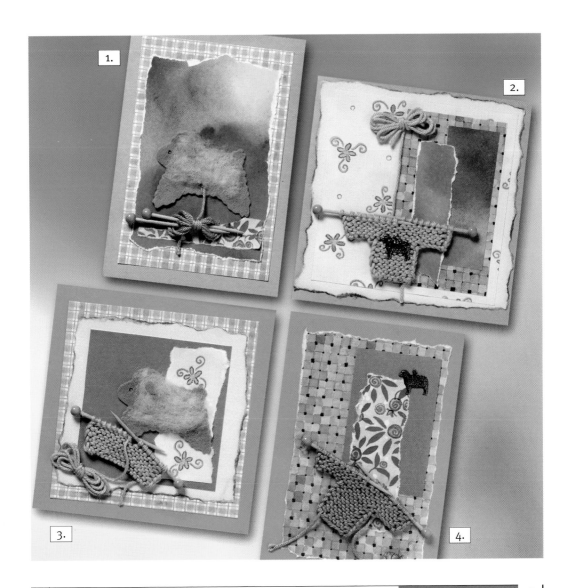

1.

2.

3.

4.

(3.5 x 7.5 cm) out of flower paper. Stick the checked paper on the card and stick the ivory card, the lilac paper and the flower paper on top. Make a sheep and stick it on the card together with a piece of pale green knitwear.

Card 4

Extra materials
❏ *Scrapbook basics: Farm animals*

Make a grass green double card (10.5 x 15 cm). Tear a rectangle (8.5 x 13 cm) out of checked paper and a strip (3 x 9 cm) out of rose paper. Cut a rectangle (5 x 8 cm) out of lilac paper. Stick the checked paper on the card and stick the lilac paper and the rose paper on top. Stick a Charm and a piece of lilac knitwear on the card.

Card 3

Extra materials
❏ *Scrap Pads: Little princess*
❏ *Felt: light grey*
❏ *Tuft of wool*
❏ *Sizzix die cutter*
❏ *Sizzix die: sheep*

Make a grass green double card (13 x 13 cm). Cut a square (11 x 11 cm) out of checked paper and a square (8.5 x 8.5 cm) out of lilac paper. Tear a square (10 x 10 cm) out of ivory card and apply chalk to the edges. Tear a strip

Roses

What you need
- ❏ *Knitwear: fuchsia (0114)*
- ❏ *Card: baby pink (C6060) and ivory (M0111)*
- ❏ *K & Company scrapbook paper: Romanza (0250 and 0260)*

Make a baby pink double card (10.5 x 15 cm). Cut a rectangle (10 x 14.5 cm) out of ivory card. Tear a rectangle (9 x 14 cm) out of vellum and apply chalk to the edges. Tear a rectangle (4 x 11 cm) out of green relief paper and wind Wire & Wire with beads around it. Tear a rectangle (3 x 7 cm) out of rose paper and apply chalk to the edges. Tear a rose out of rose paper and apply chalk to the edges. Stick the ivory card on the card and stick the vellum, the rose paper and the rose on top. Decorate the card with a piece of knitwear.

Card 1

Extra materials
- ❏ *K & Company scrapbook paper: Romanza (0252)*
- ❏ *Wire & Wire: pink (26 gauge)*
- ❏ *Beads*

Card 2

Extra materials
- ❏ *K & Company embossed stickers: Romanza (0292)*

Make a baby pink double card (13 x 13 cm). Tear a square (12.5 x 12.5 cm) out of vellum. Tear a square (11.5 x 11.5 cm) out of ivory card and apply chalk to the edges. Tear a semicircular shape out of rose paper and apply chalk to the edges. Stick the vellum on the card and stick the ivory card and the rose paper on top. Stick a butterfly and a piece of fuchsia knitwear on the card.

Card 3

Extra materials
- ❑ *K & Company scrapbook paper:*
  Romanza (0252)

Make a baby pink double card (13 x 13 cm).
Cut a square (12 x 12 cm) out of green relief
paper. Tear a square (11 x 11 cm) out of rose
paper and apply chalk to the edges. Cut four
squares (4.5 x 4.5 cm) out of ivory card and
apply chalk to the edges. Cut four roses out
of rose paper and stick them on the squares.
Stick the green paper on the card and stick
the rose paper and the squares on top. Stick
a piece of fuchsia knitwear on the card.

Card 4

Extra materials
- ❑ *K & Company embossed stickers:*
  Romanza (0292)
- ❑ *Wire & Wire: burgundy (26 gauge)*
- ❑ *Beads*

Make a baby pink double card (10.5 x 15 cm).
Cut a rectangle (9 x 14 cm) out of ivory card.
Tear a rectangle (10 x 14.5 cm) out of vellum.
Tear two rectangles (7.5 x 4.5 cm) out of rose

paper and apply chalk to the edges. Stick
the two rectangles on the ivory card and wind
Wire & Wire with beads around the ivory card.
Stick the vellum on the card and stick the ivory
card on top. Decorate the card with a butterfly
and a piece of fuchsia knitwear.

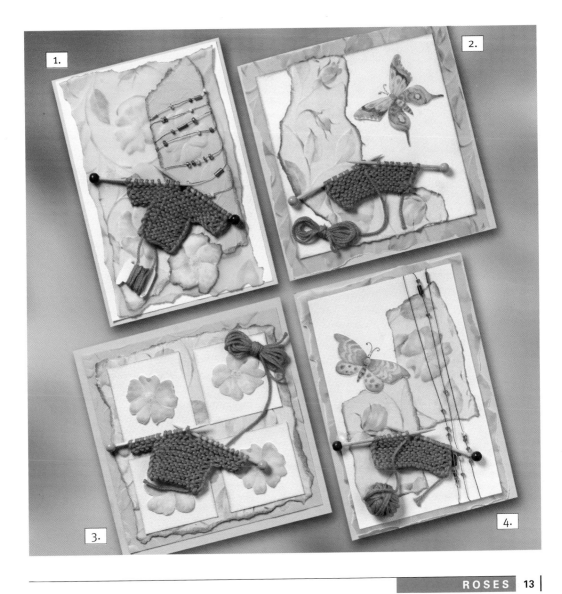

A boy and a girl

What you need
- ❏ Knitwear: wool white (0105), light blue (0103) and pale pink (0113)
- ❏ Card: light blue (C4140), bubblegum (C6110) and ivory (M0111)

Card 1

Extra materials
- ❏ K & Company scrapbook paper: Cuddly friends (0850 and 0851)
- ❏ Embellishment: baby congratulations
- ❏ Satin ribbon: pale pink
- ❏ Safety pin

Make a bubblegum double card (10.5 x 15 cm).

Cut a rectangle (10 x 14.5 cm) out of pink relief paper. Tear a rectangle (8 x 14.5 cm) out of pattern paper and apply chalk to the edges. Stick the relief paper on the card and stick the pattern paper on top. Decorate the card with a piece of wool white knitwear, embellishments and a bow made from pale pink satin ribbon.

Card 2

Extra materials
- ❏ K & Company scrapbook paper: Chelsea (0020)
- ❏ K & Company scrapbook paper: Cuddly friends (0811 and 0830)
- ❏ Embellishment: pink baby shoes
- ❏ Make Me buttons: small mix
- ❏ Satin ribbon: fuchsia

Make a bubblegum double card (13 x 13 cm). Tear a square (12 x 12 cm) out of checked paper and a square (10 x 10 cm) out of ivory card and apply chalk to the edges. Cut a square (11 x 11 cm) out of dotted paper. Stick the checked paper on the card and stick the dotted paper and the ivory card on top. Stick a button in the corners of the ivory card. Stick two flowers from the punch sheet, an embellishment and a piece of pale pink knitwear on the card.

Card 3

Extra materials
- ❑ *K & Company scrapbook paper:*
  Cuddly friends (0812, 0850 and 0852)
- ❑ *Decorative buttons: baby toys*
- ❑ *Make Me buttons: small mix*

Make a light blue double card (13 x 13 cm). Cut a square (12 x 12 cm) out of blue relief card. Tear a square (11 x 11 cm) out of striped paper and a rectangle (9 x 11 cm) out of pattern paper and apply chalk to the edges. Stick the relief paper on the card and stick the striped paper on top.

Stick a button in the corners of the pattern paper. Cut out the eye of the bear button and stick it on the card together with a piece of wool white knitwear.

Card 4

Extra materials
- ❑ *K & Company scrapbook paper:*
  Cuddly friends (0812 and 0830)
- ❑ *K & Company scrapbook paper:*
  Romanza (0213)
- ❑ *Embellishment: pastel gifts*

Make a light blue double card (10.5 x 15 cm). Tear a rectangle (10 x 14.5 cm) out of striped paper and a rectangle (8 x 12 cm) out of ivory card and apply chalk to the edges. Cut a rectangle (9 x 13 cm) out of dotted paper. Stick the striped paper on the card and stick the dotted paper and the ivory card on top. Push a dog, a moon and a duck out of the punch sheet and stick them on the card. Decorate the card with a gift and a piece of light blue knitwear.

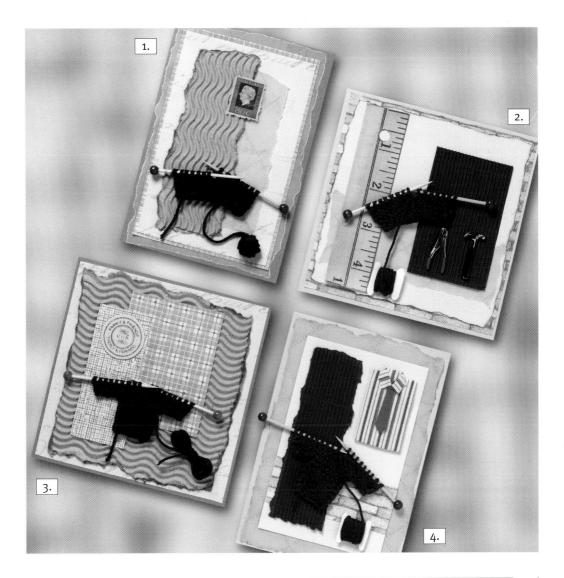

Men

What you need
- ❏ Knitwear: dark brown (0162) and dark blue (0124)
- ❏ Card: camel (C7170), light brown (C7320) and ivory (M0111)
- ❏ K & Company scrapbook paper: Isabella (0463)

Card 1

Extra materials
- ❏ Little Sizzles: Country
- ❏ K & Company scrapbook paper: Isabella (0420)
- ❏ Corrugated card: natural
- ❏ Old postage stamp

Make a light brown double card (10.5 x 15 cm). Tear a rectangle (9.5 x 14.3 cm) and a strip (3 x 10 cm) out of vellum. Cut a rectangle (9 x 13.5 cm) out of checked paper and a rectangle (8.5 x 13 cm) out of ecru pattern paper. Tear a rectangle (4 x 11.5 cm) out of corrugated card and apply chalk to the edges. Stick the large piece of vellum on the card and stick the checked paper, the ecru pattern paper, the small piece of vellum and the corrugated card on top. Decorate the card with an old postage stamp and a piece of dark blue knitwear.

Card 2

Extra materials
- ❏ Scrap Pads: River rock
- ❏ Corrugated card: blue
- ❏ Life's journey stickers: rulers
- ❏ Embellishment: tools

Make a camel double card (13 x 13 cm). Cut a square (12.5 x 12.5 cm) out of brick paper and a rectangle out of corrugated card (5 x 8 cm). Tear a square (11.5 x 11.5 cm) out of ivory card and a strip (4 x 11 cm) out of vellum. Stick the brick paper on the card and stick the ivory card,

Make a light brown double card (13 x 13 cm). Cut a square (12.5 x 12.5 cm) out of ecru pattern paper, a rectangle (6 x 8 cm) out of checked paper and a rectangle (3.5 x 8.5 cm) out of blue pattern paper. Tear a square (11.5 x 11.5 cm) out of corrugated card and apply chalk to the edges. Stick the ecru pattern paper on the card and stick the corrugated card, the checked paper and the blue pattern paper on top. Stick a round label and a piece of dark blue knitwear on the card.

Card 4

Extra materials
❏ *Scrap Pads: River rock*
❏ *Corrugated card: blue*
❏ *Embellishment: shirt*

Make a camel double card (10.5 x 15 cm). Tear a rectangle (10 x 14.5 cm) out of vellum and apply chalk to the edges. Cut a rectangle (8 x 12.5 cm) out of ivory card and a strip (3 x 8 cm) out of brick paper. Tear a strip (3.5 x 11 cm) out of corrugated card. Stick the vellum on the card and stick the ivory card, the brick paper and the corrugated card on top. Stick a shirt embellishment and a piece of dark brown knitwear on the card.

the vellum and the corrugated card on top. Stick the ruler sticker and pliers and hammer embellishment stickers on the card. Decorate the card with a piece of dark brown knitwear.

Card 3

Extra materials
❏ *K & Company scrapbook paper: Isabella (0420)*
❏ *Corrugated card: natural*
❏ *Little Sizzles: Country and Rainbow*
❏ *Life's Journey labels: round*

The beach

What you need

- *Knitwear: pale blue (0103) and soft orange (0209)*
- *Card: ivory (C7090), amber (C7330) and sand (M0407)*
- *Little Sizzles: Pastels*

Card 1

Extra materials
- *Scrap Pads: Heritage post*
- *Fun eyelet tags: open shapes*
- *Jewellery glue*

Make an amber double card (13 x 13 cm). Cut a square (12.5 x 12.5 cm) out of striped paper and a square (11.5 x 11.5 cm) out of ivory card. Tear a strip (4.5 x 11.8 cm) out of sand card, a strip (2.8 x 11 cm) out of striped paper and two strips (1 x 11.5 cm) out of blue pattern paper. Apply chalk to the edges. Stick the striped paper on the card and stick the ivory card and the torn pieces of paper on top. Stick a star eyelet tag and a piece of soft orange knitwear on the card.

Card 2

Extra materials
- *K & Company scrapbook paper: Cuddly friends (0812)*
- *Embellishment: Shell in a frame*

Make an ivory double card (10.5 x 15 cm). Cut a rectangle (5 x 8 cm) out of amber card and stick an embellishment on it. Tear a rectangle (3 x 11 cm) out of striped paper and a rectangle (2 x 8 cm) out of blue pattern paper and apply chalk to the edges. Stick the amber card, the striped paper and the pattern paper on the card. Decorate the card with a piece of pale blue knitwear.

Card 4

Extra materials
- ❏ *K & Company scrapbook paper:*
  Cuddly friends (0812)
- ❏ *Embellishment: bag of sand with shells*

Make an ivory double card (13 x 13 cm). Tear a square (12 x 12 cm) out of amber card and a square (9.5 x 9.5 cm) out of sand card and apply chalk to the edges. Cut a square (10.5 x 10.5 cm) out of striped paper. Stick the amber card on the card and stick the striped paper and the sand card on top. Stick an embellishment and a piece of pale blue knitwear on the card.

Card 3

Extra materials
- ❏ *Scrap Pads: Heritage post*
- ❏ *Embellishment: slippers*
- ❏ *Charm: travel*
- ❏ *Wire & Wire: silver (22 gauge)*
- ❏ *Jewellery glue*

Make an amber double card (10.5 x 15 cm). Tear a rectangle (9.5 x 14 cm) out of sand card and apply chalk to the edges. Tear the sky out of blue pattern paper and the beach out of striped paper. Stick the sand card on the card and stick the beach and the sky on top. Make three birds from Wire & Wire and use jewellery glue to stick them on the card. Stick a Charm suitcase and an embellishment of a pair of slippers on the card. Finally, stick a piece of soft orange knitwear on the card.

Autumn

What you need
- Knitwear: cognac (0188) and camel (0179)
- Card: tornado gold (C2090), eggshell (C7230) and ivory (M0111)
- Sharon Ann scrapbook paper: Autumn
- Scrap Pads: River rock

Card 1

Extra materials
- Embellishment: sunflower

Make an eggshell double card (10.5 x 15 cm). Cut two rectangles (9.3 x 13.8 cm and 4 x 8.8 cm) out of vellum. Tear a rectangle (4.5 x 9.5 cm) out of tornado gold card and apply chalk to the edges. Cut a rectangle (4 x 9 cm) out of checked paper. Stick the large piece of vellum on the card and stick the checked paper, the card and the small piece of vellum on top. Decorate the card with a flower and a piece of camel knitwear.

Card 2

Extra materials
- Make Me special paper: mix

Make an eggshell double card (13 x 13 cm). Tear a square (12 x 12 cm) out of tornado gold card and apply chalk to the edges. Cut a square (11.5 x 11.5 cm) out of swirl paper. Cut a rectangle (4 x 9.5 cm) out of checked paper, a rectangle (5 x 8 cm) out of ivory card and a square (3.3 x 3.3 cm) with an acorn out of vellum. Tear a rectangle (3 x 8 cm) out of fibre paper. Stick the tornado gold card on the card and stick the swirl paper, the checked paper, the ivory paper, the vellum and the fibre paper on top. Decorate the card with a piece of cognac knitwear.

the ivory paper, the checked paper and the swirl paper on top. Decorate the card with three sunflowers and a piece of cognac knitwear.

Card 4

Extra materials
❏ *Felt: moss green*

Make a tornado gold double card (10.5 x 15 cm). Cut a rectangle (10 x 14.5 cm) out of checked paper. Tear a rectangle (9 x 13 cm) out of ivory card and apply chalk to the edges. Tear a strip (4 x 13 cm) out of vellum. Cut two squares (3.3 x 3.3 cm) with an acorn out of vellum. Tear a strip (3 x 13 cm) out of felt. Stick the checked paper on the card and stick the ivory card, the two square pieces of vellum, the vellum strip and the felt strip on top. Decorate the card with a piece of camel knitwear.

Card 3

Extra materials
❏ *Little Sizzles: Watercolors*
❏ *Embellishment: sunflower*

Make a tornado gold double card (13 x 13 cm). Tear a square (12.5 x 12.5 cm) out of vellum and apply chalk to the edges. Cut a square (11.5 x 11.5 cm) out of ivory card. Tear a strip (3 x 11.5 cm) out of checked paper and swirl paper. Stick the vellum on the card and stick

1.

2.

3.

4.

Winter

What you need
- ❏ Knitwear: wool white (0105) and blue (0201)
- ❏ Card: white (C0015), sky blue (C4360) and pastel blue (C4070)
- ❏ Little Sizzles: Country
- ❏ Embellishment: snowman

Card 1

Extra materials
- ❏ Little Sizzles: Watercolors
- ❏ Angel wire: white
- ❏ Fun eyelet tags: open shapes
- ❏ Mini adhesive stones: light blue
- ❏ Felt: white

Make a sky blue double card (13 x 13 cm). Cut a square (3 x 13 cm) out of angel wire. Tear a rectangle (11 x 12 cm) out of pastel blue card and apply chalk to the edges. Cut a square (10 x 10 cm) out of blue paper. Tear a rectangle (3.5 x 10 cm) out of pattern paper and snowflake paper. Tear a square (8 x 8 cm) out of felt. Stick the angel wire on the card by applying only a small amount of glue to the middle. Stick the blue card on the card and stick the blue paper, the felt, the snowflake paper and the pattern paper on top. Stick a snowflake

eyelet tag on the felt. Stick adhesive stones on the eyelet tag. Stick a snow-man and a piece of blue knitwear on the card.

Card 2

Extra materials
- ❏ K & Company scrapbook paper: Juliana (0161)
- ❏ Eyelet shapes: blue
- ❏ Jewellery glue

Make a sky blue double card (10.5 x 15 cm). Tear a rectangle (10 x 14.5 cm) out of vellum. Cut a rectangle (9 x 13.5 cm) out of pastel blue card. Tear the ground out of grey-blue paper and the sky out of snowflake paper. Stick the vellum on the card and stick the card, the sky and the ground on top. Use jewellery glue to stick two snowflake eyelets on the card. Decorate the card with a snowman and a piece of wool white knitwear.

Card 3

Extra materials
- ❏ *Little Sizzles: Rainbow*
- ❏ *Make Me decorative frame*

Make a pastel blue double card (10.5 x 15 cm). Cut a strip (2.5 x 15 cm) and a rectangle (5.8 x 6.5 cm) out of blue paper. Tear a strip (3 x 5 cm) out of white card and a strip (3 x 9.5 cm) out of snowflake paper. Apply chalk to the edges of the torn pieces. Stick an aluminium frame on the blue rectangle. Stick the blue, white and snowflake strips on the card. Stick the rectangle with the aluminium frame on the card and stick a snowman in the frame. Decorate the card with a piece of wool white knitwear.

Card 4

Extra materials
- ❏ *Little Sizzles: Watercolors*
- ❏ *K & Company scrapbook paper: Juliana (0161)*
- ❏ *Fun eyelet tags: open shapes*
- ❏ *Mini adhesive stones: light blue*
- ❏ *Jewellery glue*

Make a pastel blue double card (13 x 13 cm). Tear a square (12.5 x 12.5 cm) and an iceberg out of vellum. Cut a square (11.3 x 11.3 cm) out of pattern paper and angel wire. Cut a strip (1.8 x 11.3 cm) out of snowflake paper. Tear a strip (4 x 10.5 cm) out of white card. Apply chalk to the torn edges of the square piece of vellum and the card. Stick the square piece of vellum on the card and stick the pattern paper, the angel wire, the snowflake strip, the iceberg and the white card on top. Stick a snowflake eyelet tag on the white felt. Stick adhesive stones on the snowflake. Have the snowman coming out from behind the iceberg. Stick a piece of blue knitwear on the card.

1.

2.

3.

4.

Christmas

What you need
- ❏ Knitwear: red (0115)
- ❏ Card: dark red (C0090),
  Christmas green (C3320) and ivory (M0111)
- ❏ Sharon Ann scrapbook paper:
  Winter

and a rectangle (5 x 10 cm) out of vellum. Tear a rectangle (8 x 12 cm) out of ivory card and apply chalk to the edges. Tear a rectangle (4 x 7.5 cm) out of green Christmas paper. Stick the checked paper on the card and stick the ivory card, the vellum and the green Christmas paper on top. Add a Bradletz. Decorate the card with a piece of red knitwear.

Card 2

Extra materials
- ❏ Bradletz: gold
- ❏ Wire & Wire: red (26 gauge)
- ❏ Beads and sequins

Make a dark red double card (13 x 13 cm). Cut a square (12 x 12 cm) out of beige Christmas paper. Tear a square (11 x 11 cm) out of ivory card and apply chalk to the edges. Tear a rectangle (3 x 10.5 cm) out of red pattern paper and a rectangle (3.5 x 8.5 cm) out of green pattern paper. Stick the red pattern paper and the green pattern paper on the ivory card and wind Wire & Wire with beads around it. Stick the beige Christmas paper on the card and stick the ivory card on top. Add a Bradletz and stick a piece of red knitwear on the card.

Card 1

Extra materials
- ❏ Bradletz: red

Make a dark red double card (10.5 x 15 cm). Cut a rectangle (9.5 x 14 cm) out of checked paper

Card 4

Extra materials
❑ *Wire & Wire: red (26 gauge)*
❑ *Beads and sequins*
Make a Christmas green double card (10.5 x 15 cm). Cut a rectangle (9.5 x 13.5 cm) out of checked paper, a rectangle (8 x 12.5 cm) out of ivory card and a rectangle (2.7 x 6.3 cm) out of red pattern paper. Tear a rectangle (3.5 x 9 cm) out of checked paper. Stick the pattern paper and the strip of checked paper on the ivory card and wind the Wire & Wire with beads around it. Stick the checked paper and the ivory card on the card. Stick a piece of red knitwear on the card.

Card 3

Extra materials
❑ *Bradletz: red*
Make a Christmas green double card (13 x 13 cm). Cut a square (12 x 12 cm) out of beige Christmas paper and a square (5 x 5 cm) out of checked paper. Tear a square (9 x 9 cm) out of ivory card and apply chalk to the edges. Tear a piece of green Christmas paper with pinecones on it. Stick the beige Christmas paper on the card and stick the card, the checked paper and the Christmas paper with pinecones on top. Add a Bradletz. Decorate the card with a piece of red knitwear.

Many thanks to Kars & Co BV in Ochten, the Netherlands. Tel: +31 (0)344-642864,
Coats B.V. in Ninove, Belgium. Tel. +32 54318989 and Brouwer in Wilnis, the Netherlands.
Tel. +31 (0)297-281557 for providing the materials.